jaico-531
4110108

C000120782

DELIGHTS
from **GOA**

DELIGHTS
from **GOA**

Aroona Reejhsinghani

JAICO PUBLISHING HOUSE

Ahmedabad Bangalore Bhopal Chennai
Delhi Hyderabad Kolkata Mumbai

Published by Jaico Publishing House
121 Mahatma Gandhi Road
Mumbai - 400 001
jaicopub@vsnl.com
www.jaicobooks.com

© Aroona Reejhsinghani

DELIGHTS FROM GOA
ISBN 81-7224-078-3

First Jaico Impression: 1987
Twelfth Jaico Impression: 2008

No part of this book may be reproduced or utilized in
any form or by any means, electronic or
mechanical including photocopying, recording or by
any information storage and retrieval system,
without permission in writing from the publishers.

Printed by
Sanman & Co.
113, Shivshakti Ind. Estate, Marol Naka
Andheri (E), Mumbai - 400 059.

Introduction

Goa nestles on the west coast of the Indian subcontinent. It is a tiny land between the Arabian Sea and the Western Ghats. It is as beautiful as a picture postcard with its palm-fringed beaches, emerald green hills and silvery rivers. Having been under Portuguese rule for over 450 years, Goan food is a mixture of both eastern and western influences. Goan hospitality is proverbial and even the unwanted guest is made welcome with a tasty meal, prepared from resources available in the house at that time. They are bon viveurs and sumptuous meals are served on every feast and other occasions like births and marriages. Goans excel in culinary art and they make such fine chefs that most of the leading hotels in India employ these chefs. I must thank Mrs. Sheila Dsouza, Jennifer Vaz and Rita Fernandes for giving me their recipes to include in this book. I hope you will like this book of mine as you have liked my many other books on regional cooking.

AROONA REEJHSINGHANI

CONTENTS

viii

Glossary

Vegetables

Ash pumpkin....*petha* or *bhopla*.
Beet....*chukander or beet*.
Bitter gourd....*karela*.
Brinjal....*baigan*.
Cluster beans.....*gavar*.
Carrots....*gajjar*.
Cauliflower....*phoolgobi*.
Cucumber....*khira*.
Capsicums....*shimla mirch*.
Corn....*makai*.
Collocasia....*arbi*.
Drumsticks.....*sheengne ki fali*.
French beans....*flas beans*.
Fenugreek leaves....*methi bhaji*.
Gherkins....*tindli*.
Green peas....*mutter*.
Green chillies....*hari mirchi*.
Green onions....*hari pyaj*.
Lotus stems....*Kamal kakdi*.
Ladies fingers....*bhendi*.
Lettuce....*salad bhaji*.
Mushrooms....*goochi*.
Mustard greens....*rai ki bhaji*.
Marrow or pumpkin....*Ghia*.
Potatoes....*alu*.
Radish....*muli*.
Rubbed gourd....*toori*.
Snake gourd....*padval*.
Sweet potatoes....*shakarkundi*.

Spinach....*palak*.
Sour lime....*limbu*.
Turnips....*Shalgum or knolkol*
Tomatoes....*tamatar*.
White gourd....*tinda*.
Water chestnuts....*Shingara*.
Yam....*Zamikand*.

Herbs

Celery....*silery*.
Corriander leaves....*dhania*.
Dill....*suva*.
Garlic....*lasoon*.
Ginger....*adhruk*.
Mint....*phudina*.

Fruits

Apple....*sev*.
Apricots....*khumani*.
Coconut....*narial*.
Custard apple....*sitaphul*.
Dates....*khajoor*.
Figs....*anjeer*.
Grapes....*angoor*.
Guava....*amroot*.
Mango....*aam*.
Olives....*jaitoon*,
Oranges....*Santra*.
Plantains....*kela*.
Pomogranate....*anar*.
Pineapple....*ananas*.

Peach....*nashpati.*
Plum....*alubhukhara.*
Watermelon....*tarbooz.*

Dry fruits

Almonds....*badam.*
Cashewnuts....*kaju.*
Dry apricots....*sukhi khumani.*
Dry coconut....*khopra.*
Dry dates....*Sukha khajoor.*
Dry figs.. *sukha anjeer.*
Dry plums....*sukha alubhukhara.*
Pistachio nuts....*pista.*
Peanuts....*moongfali.*
Raisins....*kismis.*
Walnuts....*akhrot.*

Spices

anise seeds....*sauf.*
Asafoetida....*hing.*
Bay leaf....*tejpatta.*
Basil....*cocums.*
Corriander seeds....*sukha dhania.*
Chilli powder....*pissi hui lal mirch.*
Caraway seeds....*shahjeera.*
Cardamoms....*elaychi.*
Cinnamon....*dalchini.*
Cloves....*lavang.*
Cumin seeds....*jeera.*
Dry ginger....*sunt.*

Fenugreek seeds....*methi ka beej.*
Mustard seeds....*rai.*
Nutmeg....*jaiphal.*
Pepper....*pissi hui kali mirch.*
Poppy seeds....*khus khus.*
Pomogranate seeds....*anardhana.*
Peppercorns....*sabit kala mirch.*
Mango powder....*amchoor.*
Mace....*javitri.*
Salt....*nimak.*
Sesame seeds....*til.*
Turmeric....*huldi.*
Tamrind....*imli.*
Saffron....*kesar.*

Pulses and lentils

Bengal gram....*channa ki dal.*
Black gram....*urad ki dal.*
Red gram....*masoor ki dal.*
White gram....*kabuli chana.*
Split green gram....*moong dal.*

Flours

Wheat flour....*gheun ka atta.*
Refined flour:....*maida.*
Maize flour....*makai ka atta.*
Semolina....*sooji or rava.*
Gram flour....*besan.*

Sweets & Desserts

1

Rava Burfi

1 cup rava or semolina.
1 cup ghee.
1 cup finely grated coconut.
1 cup milk.
2 cups sugar.
A few drops essence of saffron.
1 tblsp. powdered cardamoms.
10 each of almonds, pistachios and cashewnuts.

Pound together all the nuts coarsely. Put the rest of the ingredients together in a pan and cook stirring all the time till the mixture turns thick and leaves the sides of the vessel. Mix in the essence and remove from fire, put in a greased thali, level the surface and sprinkle nuts on the top. Cool thoroughly, cut into small squares and store in airtight container.

2

Guava Cheese

500 grams ripe guavas.
500 grams sugar.
1 tblsp. butter.
25 grams mixed nuts like almonds, pistachios and charoli.
Juice of 1 lime.

Peel guavas and dice them. Mix in lime juice and place them over a slow fire. Cover tightly and cook without adding water till the guavas turn very soft. Remove from fire, mash to a paste and pass through a fine sieve and discard all the seeds. Put 2 cups water in sugar and prepare a syrup of one-thread consistency. Put in the rest of the above ingredients and keep on cooking till the mixture can not be moved with the spoon. Remove from fire and put in a shallow greased thali. Level the surface, cool nicely and cut into small pieces. Wrap each piece in butter paper and store in airtight container.

3

Bole Cake

3 coconuts.
12 egg yolks.
8 egg whites.
1 kilo sugar.
½ kilo semolina.
1 tblsp. powdered cardamom seeds.
Rose water.
125 grams ghee.

Lightly roast the semolina. Scrape and grind the coconuts to a very fine and smooth paste in rose water. Put ½ litre water into the sugar and prepare a syrup of one-thread consistency. Remove from fire and cool. Mix together cardamoms, syrup, coconut, semolina ghee and yolks. Beat till stiff and fold into the mixture. Apply ghee nicely on a baking tin, pour in the mixture and bake in a moderate oven for 15 to 20 minutes, or till a toothpick inserted in the centre comes out clean.

4

Neuris

500 grams refined flour.
1 cup ghee.
3 tblsps. cornflour.
Pinch of salt.

Filling....300 grams semolina. 300 grams powdered or ground sugar. 25 grams each of almonds, pistachios, cashewnuts and charoli. 1 coconut, finely grated. 100 grams raisins. 2 tblsps. poppy seeds. 1 tblsp. cardamom seeds. $\frac{1}{4}$ tsp. grated nutmeg.

Mix cornflour with a little ghee to form thin and smooth paste. Mix together salt and flour and rub in the remaining ghee, then pour in enough water to form a dough of medium consistency. Cover and set aside. Fry all the nuts to a golden colour, then pound them coarsely with cardamoms. Also fry the coconut and poppy seeds to a golden colour. Fry raisins also to a golden colour and also fry semolina in 6 tblsps. ghee to a golden colour. Remove from fire and mix in all the fried ingredients along with sugar and jaiphal and set aside. Divide the dough into lime-sized balls and roll out each ball into a round disc or chapati. Apply cornflour paste over each chapati and sandwich about 5 of them. The last one should be clean, then roll them out again into one big round without breaking it. Stamp out rounds with the help of a biscuit cutter or an inverted glass. Put a little filling on one half of the round, fold over the other half to form a crescent and seal and crimp the edges together. Deep fry on both the sides to a cream colour. Drain thoroughly, cool and store in airtight containers.

5

Baath

500 grams semolina.
250 grams butter.
6 big eggs, separated.
½ kilo powdered sugar.
2 coconuts.
½ tsp. baking powder.
A pinch of salt.
1 tsp. either essence of rose or vanilla.

For pastry....125 grams refined flour. 1 tblsp. butter.
Sift the flour together with baking powder and salt.
Scrape and grind the coconuts to a very smooth and fine
paste. Cream the butter and sugar together. Add the
yolks to the creamed mixture one at a time, beating
thoroughly after each addition. Beat the whites till they
stand up in stiff peaks. Add to the mixture alternatively
with flour mixture beating thoroughly after each addition. Mix in the coconut and essence and set aside
whole night. The next morning, if you find the mixture
stiff, put in a little milk to soften it. Put the mixture
in well-greased and flat baking tins and level out the
surface. Now take flour and rub in butter, add enough
water to form a soft dough. Roll out the dough into a

8

not too thin round and then cut into long strips about 1-inch thick. Roll each strip into a tight roll lengthwise. Arrange the strips of rolled strips on top of each baath in lattice work. Bake in a moderate oven for 15 to 20 minutes, or until a toothpick inserted in the centre comes out clean.

6

Bolo Gostoso

500 grams semolina or rava.
1½ coconuts.
1 tsp. cardamom seeds.
½ wineglass wine.
750 grams sugar.
50 grams mixed sliced nuts like cashewnuts, almonds and raisins.
6 eggs, separated.
1 tsp. vanilla essence.

Grind the coconut to a paste. Put sugar, 3 tblsps. butter and cardamoms over a slow fire and cook till the mixture turns into a syrup. Cool slightly and mix in semolina, nuts and essence. Set aside 1 hour. Beat the yolks and mix in along with wine. Then fold in the stiffly beaten egg whites. Grease and flour a shallow baking tray, put in the mixture and bake to a light golden colour. If you like you can arrange whole nuts on top of the batter in any design you like before putting it to bake.

7

Beveca

1 cup each of refined flour and semolina.
Thick coconut milk.
25 grams blanched and sliced almonds.
125 grams butter.
250 grams sugar.
1 tsp. essence of almond or rose.
1 tsp. caraway seeds.

Cream the butter and sugar together then beat in the eggs one at a time. Mix in the flour, semolina and caraway seeds. Mix in the essence and enough coconut milk to form a thick batter. Put in a greased glass oven ware dish and bake in a moderate oven till golden and firm. Test by inserting a toothpick in the centre if it comes out clean then remove from the oven otherwise bake a little longer.

8

Kul Kuls

500 grams semolina.
500 grams sugar.
1 tsp. essence of rose.
3 eggs.
30 grams butter.
1 tsp. coarsely pounded cardamom seeds.
Thick coconut milk.

Rub butter into semolina. Add cardamoms and enough coconut milk to form a stiff dough. Put 1 cup water in sugar and prepare a thick syrup. Remove from fire. Mix in essence and keep it warm. Divide the dough into small balls. Flatten out each ball on a greased fork and roll it backwards firmly leaving the lines of the fork on the outside. Deep fry to a golden brown colour. Drain and toss into the syrup. When the syrup begins to dry, separate the kul kuls from each other and place on a clean plate. Store in airtight containers when cold. After getting cold they should have a hard sugary layer on the surface. You can also make buds, flowers and animals from this dough.

9

Special Goan Cakes

1 kilo semolina.
12 eggs.
3 coconuts.
500 grams sugar.
1 tblsp. caraway seeds.
1/8 tsp. salt.
4 tblsps. butter.

Roast the semolina on a girdle without butter to a golden colour; Add 1 cup water to sugar and prepare a thick syrup. Grind the coconuts to a paste. Separate the eggs. Use only the yolks and keep the whites for any other called for recipe. Beat the yolks and mix into the cooled sugar syrup. Mix in the remaining ingredients. Form the mixture into a dough. Divide the dough into small, round and flat cakes. Arrange on greased tray and bake in a moderate oven till done.

10

Bolina

2 cups semolina.
2 cups powdered cashewnuts.
yolks of 6 eggs.
3 ground coconuts.
Ground sugar equal to the weight of ground coconuts.
½ tsp. vanilla essence,

Mix together all the ingredients with the exception of coconut. Set aside whole night. Add the coconut. Put spoonfuls of mixtures in greased patty tins and bake in a moderate oven till done.

11

Bibique

12 egg yolks only.
500 grams each of sugar and refined flour.
125 grams ghee.
4 cups thick coconut milk.
1/8 tsp. salt.
½ tsp. powdered nutmeg.

Put 1 cup water in sugar and prepare a thick syrup. Beat the eggs and mix into the cooled sugar syrup along with the rest of the above ingredients. Keep on mixing the batter till it is smooth. Take a deep ovenware dish and put in 1 tblsp. ghee. When it is heated pour 1 cup of batter in it. Level the surface and bake in a moderate oven till it is firm. Now pour 1 tblsp. ghee on top and pour another cupful of batter on top. Level the surface and put in the oven again. Bake again till it is firm. Continue in this way till all the batter is used up. You can colour the different layer differently and have a ribben cake.

12

Gram Sweet

2 cups gram dal.
3 cups sugar.
1 coconut, ground to a paste.
3 tblsps. ghee.
1 tsp. cardamom seeds.

Boil the gram dal till soft and mash to a paste and pass through a sieve. Put 1 cup water and cardamoms in sugar and make a thick syrup. Add the rest of the ingredients and keep on stirring till the mixture turns thick and leaves the sides of the vessel. Put on a greased slab, level the surface and cover with silver foil if you like. Cut into pieces when cold.

13

Pasteis da sta clara

250 grams refined flour.
1 tblsp. butter.
A big pinch salt.
Icing sugar.

For the filling....125 grams sugar. 6 egg yolks. 125 grams chopped cashewnuts. 125 grams potatoes, boiled, peeled and mashed. ½ tsp. almond essence.

Mix together flour, salt, butter. Add enough water to form a stiff dough. Add 1 cup water to sugar and prepare a thick syrup. Put in nuts and egg yolks stirring all the time till the mixture turns thick. Add mashed potatoes. Mix well and add the essence. Divide the dough into small balls. Roll out each ball into a thin round. Place a portion of the filling on one-half of the round and fold over to form halfmoon shapes. Seal and crimp the edges together—Deep fry to a golden colour and roll nicely in icing sugar.

14

Marzipan

2 cups cashewnuts.
2 cups sugar—colours and essences of choice.

Grind the cashewnuts to a fine paste with little water,
melt sugar, add cashewnuts and keep on stirring till the
mixture leaves the sides of the pan. Put in essence and
remove from fire. Put the mixture over a greased slab
and knead to a smooth mixture. Add colours of your
choice and form into flowers, fruits or animals of your
choice.

15

Coconut Pancakes

2 cups refined flour or maida.
3 eggs.
Pinch of salt.
2 tblsps. sugar.
1 tblsp. ghee.
1 cup thick coconut milk
½ cup milk.

For the filling....2 large coconuts, scraped. 1½ cups sugar.
1 tblsp. crushed cardamom seeds.

Mix together salt and flour. Beat the eggs with sugar.
Add the milks. Put the mixture in the flour gradually
stirring all the time. Mix in the ghee and set aside for
half an hour. Put the coconut, sugar and cardamoms
on a slow fire and cook till the mixture turns thick.
Heat a pan nicely, put in little ghee, then put 2 table-
spoons of batter on the pan and spread to a thin round.
Fry on both the sides to a light golden colour. Put
coconut filling in each pancake—and roll up.

16

Flaming Banana Fritters

2 tblsps. refined flour.
1 egg.
Milk.
1 banana, peeled.
1 tblsp. orange marmalade.
2 tblsps. orange juice.
1 tblsp. brandy.

Beat the egg nicely, mix in the flour then add enough milk to form a thick batter. Cut banana into thin and long slices. Dip the slices in batter and deep fry to a golden colour. Put fritters in a serving plate. Mix marmalade and orange juice. Melt 1 tsp. butter, add the marmalade mixture and blend thoroughly. Pour over banana pieces. Just before serving heat brandy light with a match and while the brandy is still flaming pour over the fritters. Serve at once.

17

Special Gram Toffee

750 grams gram dal.
750 grams semolina.
1½ coconut, grated.
1½ kilo sugar.
300 grams butter.
250 grams cashewnuts, sliced finely.
½ tsp. grated nutmeg.
1 tsp. essence of rose.
8 eggs, separated.
1/8 tsp. salt.

Cream butter and sugar together. Beat the eggs and mix in the sugar mixture. Gradually add the semolina. Mix till smooth. Boil the dal and grind to a paste. Also grind coconut to a paste. Mix together all the above ingredients and put in a greased ovenware dish. Decorate the top with whole cashewnuts and bake in a moderate oven till done.

18

Coconut Cream Toffee

3 cups cream.
4 cups sugar.
1 large coconut, ground to a paste.
1 tsp. cardamom seeds.
½ tsp. essence of rose.

Mix together all the above ingredients and put in a pan. keep on stirring till the mixture leaves the sides of the pan. Put on a greased slab. Cut into pieces when cold and store in airtight tin.

19

Banana Puffs

1 cup refined flour or maida.
Pinch of salt.
Dash of baking soda.
1 tblsp melted butter.
Buttermilk.
2 ripe bananas.
2 tblsps. grated coconut.
¼ tsp. grated nutmeg and ground cardamoms.
Icing sugar.

Mix together flour, salt, soda and butter. Add enough buttermilk to form a stiff dough. Peel and mash the bananas. Mix in the coconut and spices. Form the dough into a ball and roll out into a thin sheet on a flavoured board. Cut into small rounds with an inverted wine glass. Place spoonfuls of banana mixture in the centre of half of the rounds. Cover each filled round with the remaining rounds and seal and pinch the edges together. Deep fry to a golden colour. Drain and dust with icing sugar.

20

Coconut Cashewnut Toffee

1 kilo finely grated coconut.
500 grams cream.
750 grams sugar.
1 tsp. essence of rose.
250 grams ground cashewnuts.
2 tsps. cardamom seeds.
A few whole each of fried cashewnuts and raisins.

Melt sugar and prepare a thick syrup. Add cream along with the rest of the above ingredients with the exception of whole nuts and essence. Keep on stirring till the mixture leaves the sides of the pan. Mix in the essence and remove from fire. Divide into half. Colour one part into a light pink colour. Spread white portion on a greased slab. Level the surface and spread pink on top. Level the surface again and decorate with nuts and raisins. Set aside to turn cold and cut into pieces. Store in airtight tin.

21

Banana Toffee

2 cups peeled and mashed ripe bananas.
1½ cups cream.
3 tblsps. finely sliced mixed nuts.
Sugar to taste.
2 tblsps. butter.
¼ tsp. cardamoms.
A few drops essence of rose.

Melt sugar and mix in the rest of the above ingredients with the exception of nuts. Cook till it leaves the sides of the pan. Put on a greased slab and decorate with nuts. Cut into pieces when cold.

22

Doldol

2 coconuts.
500 grams rice flour.
500 grams Goa palm jaggery.

Grind the coconuts and extract 3 cups thin milk and thick milk. Mix flour with thin milk. Heat it adding jaggery and 1/8 tsp. salt. When the mixture bubbles. add the thick coconut milk gradually stirring all the time. When the mixture turns thick and leaves the sides of the pan remove from fire. Put in a buttered dish and smoothen with a greased plantain leaf. When cold cut into pieces. You can add in it fried and chopped cashewnuts and raisins. And also cardamom seeds and grated nutmeg would go well with it.

23

Sanas

500 grams rice flour.
2 cups thick coconut milk.
1/3 cup good toddy.
Salt or sugar to taste.

Mix together all the above ingredients to a batter. Grease the cups of idli stand. Put 1 large cup of water in the pressure cooker. Fill the cups of idli stand with batter and place the stand in the cooker. Close the lid, do not use the regulator for making the Sanas. They will be ready within 15 minutes. If the sanas are wanted sweet put in sugar if not salt. They are usually taken with meat and fish curries. They are usually made in a chatty, but they come out equally good in an idli stand.

24

Teglinhas de Conde

For the pastry mould....

250 grams refined flour or maida.
1 tblsp. melted butter.
Pinch of salt.

For filling....

5 egg whites.
1½ cups sugar.
¼ tsp. essence of almonds.
100 grams chopped cashewnuts.
50 grams chopped raisins.
Lime juice to taste.

Mix together the pastry ingredients. Add enough water
to knead to a soft but firm dough. Roll out into a thin
sheet. Cut into small pieces and line small boat-shaped
moulds which should be lightly buttered. Prick the
bottom of the pastry. Beat whites, fold in sugar and
beat again. Mix in the rest of the filling ingredients.
Half fill the moulds with the filling and bake in a moderate oven till golden brown.

25

Mango Phool

2 green mangoes.
4 cups chilled milk.
Cracked ice.
Few drops essence of rose.
4 tblsps. sugar.

Cut the mangoes into pieces. Boil in 4 cups water till soft. Pass through a sieve and strain through a cloth. Add sugar to sweeten the liquid, Chill and mix with the rest of the above ingredients. Serve with cracked ice.

26

Orchata

500 grams almonds.
400 grams sugar.
2 bottles water.
1 tsp. essence of rose.
10 cardamoms.
½ cup milk.

Pound cardamoms to a fine powder. Grind almonds to a paste after blanching them. Tie cardamoms in a piece of cloth. Put sugar and water in a pan. Put in spice bag and boil gently till the sugar dissolves. Mix in milk. Remove scum as it rises to the surface. Put in the almonds. When the syrup begins to thicken remove from fire. When cold squeeze out the juice from the spice bag and discard it. Mix in the essence and strain out through a fine cloth. Bottle and cork. When you want to drink it, place a tblsp. of the syrup in a glass, fill with cold water. It is a very delicious drink. Use strained almonds in any other recipe.

Fish & Prawns

2 tblsps. oil and fry onions, sliced chillies and remaining sliced ginger to a brown colour. Put in the remaining paste, salt, tomatoes and sugar and cook till the
tomatoes feel soft. Put in the fish and then thin milk
and cook over a slow fire till the fish are cooked. Pour
in the thick milk. Heat to simmering and serve. Garnish with corriander leaves.

27

Assag

1 medium white-fleshed fish.
1 tblsp. each of corriander and poppy seeds.
½ tsp. cumin seeds.
1 tsp. rice.
A few corriander leaves.
Refined flour.
12 cashewnuts.
2 medium onions, finely sliced.
A big pinch sugar.
½ coconut.
2 green chillies, slitted.
4 medium tomatoes, peeled and sliced.
1 tsp. turmeric powder.
Salt and chilli powder to taste.

Apply salt and turmeric powder on fish and set aside for
15 minutes. Roll lightly in flour and deep fry till light
golden in colour. Grind corriander, poppy and cumin
seeds, peppercorns, 4 flakes garlic rice, coconut and
cashewnuts to a paste. Extract juice....this is known
as a thick milk. Pour 2 cups hot water over the squeezed out pulp and set aside for 15 minutes, then squeeze
the pulp dry... this is known as the thin milk. Heat

2 tblsps. oil and fry onions, ginger, chillies and remaining sliced ginger to a brown colour. Put in the remaining spices, salt, tomatoes and sugar and cook till the tomatoes turn soft. Put in the fish and then thin milk and cook over a slow fire till the fish is cooked. Pour in the thick milk, heat to simmering and serve hot decorated with corriander leaves.

28

Fried Mackrel

6 mackrels.
4 red chillies.
2 flakes garlic.
1 small piece ginger.
½ tsp. sugar.
1 tsp. cumin seeds.
½ tsp. peppercorns.
1 medium onion.
1 tsp. vinegar.
1 tblsp. tamrind juice.
½ tsp. turmeric powder.
Salt to taste
Semolina or Bread crumbs.

Clean, wash and keep the fish whole. Grind together the remaining ingredients to a smooth paste with vinegar. Slit the fish on one side and stuff with ground mixture. Roll either in semolina or crumbs and shallow fry to a golden colour. Serve hot.

Pomfret Curry

1 pomfret.
½ coconut.
1 tblsp. cumin seeds.
3 red chillies.
A few curry leaves.
2 tblsps. each of corriander and poppy seeds.
1 large onion.
4 green chillies, slitted.
3 cocums.
4 flakes garlic.
10 cashewnuts.
1 lime-sized ball of tamrind.
Salt to taste.

Clean and cut the fish into slices. Apply salt and turmeric powder on it. Set aside for 15 minutes then fry
it lightly. Roast together onion red chillies, garlic, coconut, corriander, cumin and poppy seeds and grind to
a paste along with tamarind. Heat 3 tblsps. oil and fry
the paste nicely, adding water from time to time till a
nice aroma comes out of the mixture. Pour in 3 cups
water and cocums and bring to a boil, place the slices
of fish in it and cook till the fish is done and gravy little
thick. Serve decorated with corriander-leaves.

Fish and Brinjal Curry

1 pomfret or any other white-fleshed fish.
250 grams brinjals, cut into long thick slices.
1 lime-sized ball of tamrind.
1 tbsp. mustard seeds.
1 big onion sliced.
1 tblsp. corriander seeds.
1 tsp. each of cumin seeds and turmeric powder.
1 tblsp. poppy seeds.
6 flakes garlic.
6 red chillies.
1-inch piece ginger.
1 medium onion.
½ coconut.
Salt to taste.

Clean and cut the fish into slices. Apply salt and turmeric powder on it and set aside for 15 minutes. Roast
together corriander, cumin and poppy seeds, 1 medium
onion, ginger, garlic, chillies and coconut and grind to
a fine paste. Fry the fish lightly in oil. Soak the tamarind in 1 cup hot water for 5 minutes and then squeeze
out the juice. Heat 2 tblsps. oil and put in the mustard
seeds. When they stop popping, put in the onion and

fry till soft. Put in the ground paste and fry till a beautiful aroma comes out of the mixture. Put in tamrind and 3 cups water and bring to a boil. Reduce heat to simmering and put in the brinjals and fish. Cover tightly and cook till both the fish and vegetable is done. Serve with plain boiled rice.

31

Baked Fish

1 kilo fish.
½ coconut.
1 cup thick coconut milk.
2 medium onions.
6 flakes garlic.
1-inch piece ginger.
6 red chillies.
1 tsp. cumin seeds.
1 tblsp. corriander seeds.
1 tsp. garam masala.
½ tsp. turmeric powder.
1 tblsp. vinegar.
1 tsp. sugar.
2 big tomatoes, peeled and sliced.
Salt to taste.

Apply turmeric and salt on fish slices. Grind coconut, onions, garlic, ginger, chillies all the spices to a paste. Heat 2 tblsps. oil and fry tomatoes till soft. Add the rest of the above ingredients and mix well. Apply on the slices of fish and put in a greased ovenware dish. Bake in a moderate oven till cooked. Decorate with corriander leaves.

32

Stuffed Fish

5 mackerels.
2 medium onions.
10 peppercorns.
1 lime-sized ball of tamrind.
1 tsp. garam masala.
3 flakes garlic.
1-inch piece ginger.
1 tsp. sugar.
1 tsp. ground cumin seeds.
Salt to taste.

Clean Mackerel and slit belly. Make gashes on the top.
Roast the onions for 10 minutes. Peel and grind to a
thin paste with the rest of the above ingredients with the
exception of fish. Mix with 1 tblsp. oil and stuff nicely
into the fish. Roll in semolina or bread crumbs and
shallow fry to a golden colour. Serve with raw onion
and lime.

33

Baked Mackrel

6 mackrels.
½ coconut.
1 large onion.
2 green chillies.
6 red chillies.
½ tsp. turmeric powder.
lime-sized ball of tamrind.
4 flakes garlic.
½-inch piece ginger.
½ cup corriander leaves.
Salt to taste.

Chop onion, chillies and ginger. Grind the rest of the above ingredients to a paste. Mix in 4 tblsps. oil. Spread half of the mixture in a baking dish, place mackerel on top and spread the rest of the mixture on top. Bake in a moderate oven for 15 minutes.

34

Fish Caldeen

1 kilo fish cleaned and sliced.
100 grams ladies fingers, cut into 2-inch pieces, fried in oil till crisp.
2 medium onions, sliced.
2 green chillies, slitted.
1 tblsp. corriander seeds.
1 lime-sized ball of tamrind.
½ tsp. each of cumin seeds and turmeric powder.
12 peppercorns.
4 flakes garlic.
6 red chillies.
½ coconut, grated.

Grind whole spices, garlic, chillies and coconut to a paste. Cover tamrind with hot water for 5 minutes and then squeeze out the juice. Apply salt and turmeric on fish and set aside for 15 minutes. Fry lightly. Heat 3 tblsps. oil and fry onions to a light golden colour. Add the spices and fry till a nice aroma comes out of it. Put in the fish, cover with water and cook till the fish is almost done. Put in the chillies and vegetable and tamrind. When the fish is cooked and the gravy quite thick remove from fire.

Fish in Tomato Sauce

1 medium pomfret, cut into pieces.
4 red chillies.
1 tsp. cumin seeds.
6 flakes garlic.
½ tsp. turmeric powder.
1 medium onion.
2 large tomatoes, peeled and chopped.
1 tblsp. tamrind juice.
A big pinch sugar.
Salt to taste.
Handful of corriander leaves.
½-inch piece ginger.

Grind chillies, cumin seeds and garlic to a paste. Heat 3 tblsps. oil and fry onion and ginger to a light golden colour. Add the ground spices and fry well. Put in the tomatoes, salt, tamrind and rest of the spices. Fry well. Add the fish, cover with water and cook till the fish is tender and gravy thick. Decorate with corriander leaves.

Special Prawn Curry

500 grams prawns, cleaned.
6 red chillies.
1 large onion.
1 tblsp. corriander seeds.
1 tsp. turmeric powder.
1 tsp. cumin seeds.
6 flakes garlic.
½ coconut.
1-inch piece ginger.
2 green chillies.
1 small raw mango, sliced or
1 lime-sized ball of tamrind.
Salt to taste.

Slit green chillies. Grind together the remaining ingredients to a fine paste with the exception of mango and prawns. Heat 3 tblsps. oil and add onion. Fry till it starts changing colour. Put in the ground paste and fry till a nice aroma comes out of it. Put in the prawns and cook till the mixture turnsdry. Pour in 3 cups water, bring to a boil. Reduce heat to simmering and put in the pieces of mangoes and chillies. Cook till the prawns turn tender. Serve with boiled rice.

Prawn Masala Fry

500 grams prawns, cleaned.
1 huge onion, minced.
4 flakes garlic.
1 tsp. each of turmeric powder and powdered cumin seeds.
¼ finely grated coconut.
2 tblsps. tamrind juice.
Handful corriander leaves.
Salt and chilli powder to taste.

Grind garlic and rub on the prawns together with salt
and turmeric. Heat 4 tblsps. oil and fry onions till soft.
Put in the prawns and fry to a golden colour. Put in
the rest of the above ingredients and cook over a slow
fire till the prawns are tender and dry. Decorate with
corriander leaves.

Prawn Balchao

500 grams prawns, cleaned.
¼ cup vinegar.
10 red chillies.
4 medium onions.
6 flakes garlic.
1-inch piece ginger.
1 tsp. cumin seeds.
10 peppercorns.
4 green chillies, slitted.
A few sprigs curry leaves
½ tsp. turmeric powder.
Salt to suit the taste.

Grind all the whole spices, red chillies and garlic in vinegar. Apply salt and turmeric on prawns. Heat 3 tblsps. oil and fry the ginger & onions to a light golden colour. Add the prawns and the rest of the above ingredients and cook till tender and dry. Serve hot with rice.

39

Prawn Baffad

500 grams prawns, cleaned.
8 red chillies.
½ tsp. each of cumin seeds and peppercorns and turmeric
powder.
3 flakes garlic.
½-inch piece ginger.
2 medium onions.
1 big tomato, peeled and sliced.
2 tblsps. vinegar.
1 tblsp. tamrind juice.
Salt to taste.

Apply salt and turmeric on the prawns. Grind in vinegar all the whole spices. Heat 4 tblsps. oil and add the
onions, ginger and garlic. Fry to a light golden colour.
Add the prawns and cook till dry. Add the rest of the
above ingredients. Cook over a slow fire till the prawns
are cooked. Serve hot.

40

Prawn Curry

500 grams prawns, cleaned.
1 tsp. each of cumin and corriander seeds.
4 flakes garlic.
A big pinch sugar.
½ tsp. turmeric powder.
2 medium onions, sliced.
1 lime-sized ball of tamrind.
½ coconut.
6 red chillies.
Salt to taste.

Extract thick and thin milk from the coconut. Slice garlic. Heat 3 tblsps. oil and fry onions and garlic till soft and golden. Add all the ground spices and red ground chillies and sugar and Mix well. Put in the prawns and fry till dry. Put in the thin milk. When the prawns are almost done. Add tamrind and cook till the prawns are done. Pour in thick milk, heat to simmering and remove from fire. Serve decorated with corriander leaves.

41

Prawns in Hot Chilli Sauce

500 grams prawns, cleaned.
250 grams tomatoes, sliced.
½ tsp. turmeric powder.
5 flakes garlic.
½-inch piece ginger.
1 tsp. each of cumin seeds and garam masala.
8 red chillies.
½ cup vinegar.
Salt to taste.

Grind ginger, garlic, chillies and cumin seeds to a paste.
Heat 3 tblsps oil and fry the ground paste nicely. Add
the tomatoes and the rest of the spices and cook till
thick. Put in the prawns, vinegar and cover with water.
Cook till the prawns are tender and gravy thick.

Prawn and Curd Curry

1 kilo prawns, cleaned.
10 red chillies.
½ tsp. turmeric powder.
10 peppercorns.
½ coconut, grated.
4 green chillies, slitted.
A few curry leaves.
½-inch piece ginger.
Salt to suit the taste.
1 tsp. cumin seeds.
1 tsp. garam masala.

Grind chillies, coconut and whole spices to a paste. Apply salt and turmeric powder on the prawns and set aside for 15 minutes. Heat 4 tblsps. oil add onions, ginger and curry leaves and cook till soft. Add the ground paste and continue cooking till a nice aroma comes out of the mixture. Add the prawns. When the mixture turns dry, put in well-beaten curds blended with ½ cup water. Cook till the prawns are tender and gravy thick. Serve with boiled rice.

Pickles & Chutneys

43

Pork Serpotel

2 kilos pork.
20 red chillies.
1 tblsp. cumin seeds.
1 tsp. mustard seeds.
1 tblsp. turmeric powder.
7 cloves.
10 peppercorns.
1-inch piece cinnamon stick.
¾ bottle vinegar.
6 flakes garlic.
2-inch piece ginger.
5 green chillies.
Salt to taste.

Grind all the spices to a fine paste in a little vinegar.
Cut pork into small pieces. Do not wash in water.
Wash in a little vinegar and place in a vessel. Cover
tightly and let it cook in it's own juice till dry. Add 6
tblsps. of oil and fry to a golden colour. Add the
ground paste and cook till the oil floats to the top. Add
vinegar and cook stirring often till the pork is tender.
Cool thoroughly and store in airtight bottle.

44

Prawn Ballchow No. 1

500 grams prawns, cleaned and washed in vinegar not
    water.
10 red chillies
1-inch piece ginger.
12 flakes garlic.
10 peppercorns.
500 grams onions.
3 green chillies.
10 big tomatoes peeled and sliced.
¼ large bottle of sweet oil.
1 tblsp. turmeric powder.
Salt to taste.

Grind onions, green chillies and ginger to a paste. Grind
separately garlic and all the dry spices to a paste. Heat
oil add onions and fry till brown. Add garlic paste and
fry till a nice aroma comes out of it. Add prawns and
cook till dry. Add tomatoes and salt and cook stirring
often till the prawns are tender. Cool and store in airtight bottles.

Prawn Ballchow No. 2

500 grams prawns, cleaned and washed in vinegar not
water.
12 flakes garlic.
6 red chillies.
2 tsps. cumin seeds.
5 small onions, minced.
1½ cups vinegar.
A couple of curry leaves.
1 tsp. turmeric powder.
Salt to taste.

Grind garlic, chillies and cumin seeds to a paste, apply
salt and turmeric on prawns and fry in 8 tblsps. sweet
oil till crisp and golden. Drain prawns. In the same
oil fry onions to a light golden colour. Put in the ground
paste and fry till a nice aroma comes out of it. Put in
curry leaves, prawns and vinegar. When the prawns
turn tender and mixture thick remove from fire. Put in
an airtight container.

Fish Pudda

1½ kilo white fleshed fish.
500 grams tamrind.
4 cups vinegar.
250 grams ginger.
20 flakes garlic.
75 grams red chillies.
4 tblsps. cumin seeds.
Handful of peppercorns.
2 tblsps. turmeric powder.

Grind dry spices with the exception of peppercorns to a paste with garlic and ginger in vinegar. Cut fish into thick slices. Wash in vinegar, cover with salt and set aside for 24 hours. Cover the tamrind with 4 cups vinegar and set aside for 5 hours. Make a thick paste of tamrind and vinegar with your hands and pass through a sieve. Remove the fish from the brine, wipe dry with a clean cloth, then rub both the sides of the fish well with the ground masala paste. Pour tamrind into a wide-mouthed jar, sufficient to cover the bottom. Place a layer of fish slice on it and cover with another thick layer of tamrind pulp. Layer fish and tamrind till the whole mixture is used up. Then scatter peppercorns on top and pour in enough vinegar to cover the whole. Cork the jar tightly and sun for 1 month regularly. Shake the jar as often as possible during this time. When wanted for use, fry the slices in ghee or oil till crisp and brown.

47

Dry Fish Chutney

250 grams any dry fish of your choice.
6 red chillies.
1 tblsp. each of cumin seeds and peppercorns.
1 tsp. turmeric powder.
lime-sized ball of tamrind.
Salt to taste.

Roast the fish to a red colour and grind to a paste with
the rest of the above ingredients. Serve with curry and
rice.

48

Dry Prawn Chutney

1 cup dried prawns.
3 red chillies.
1 medium onion.
½ coconut grated.
1 tblsp. oil.

Roast the prawns to a red colour and grind to a coarse
paste with all the above ingredients. Mix in the oil and
if you like a little lime juice.

Dry Prawn Ballchow

500 grams dried prawns.
100 grams tamrind.
250 grams bilimbi.
12 sour limes.
½ bottle sweet oil.
8 red chillies.
1 tsp. cumin seeds.
1 tsp. turmeric powder.
12 green chillies.
2-inch piece ginger.
18 flakes garlic.
Salt to taste.

Grind in vinegar chillies, ginger, garlic and cumin seeds. Cover the tamrind with lime juice and set aside for a few hours. Mash to a pulp with your hands and pass through a sieve. Heat oil to smoking, add the prawns and fry till red. Put in the rest of the above ingredients and cook till thick. Cool and bottle.

50

Egg Pickle

12 hard-boiled eggs, shelled.
3 cups vinegar.
1-inch piece cinnamon stick.
12 cloves.
1 tblsp. coarsely pounded mustard seeds.
12 peppercorns.
6 red chillies.
4 flakes garlic.
1-inch piece ginger.
Salt to taste.
½ tsp. sugar.

Grind ginger and garlic. Mix together all the above ingredients with the exception of eggs and boil for 15 minutes. Strain and cool. Pack eggs in a jar and pour the vinegar on top. Cover tightly and use after a week. They can be used in salads or sandwiches.

51

Beef Pickle

½ *kilo beef.*
6 red chillies.
1 tsp. each of cumin seeds and turmeric powder.
½ *tsp. mustard seeds.*
12 peppercorns.
6 flakes garlic.
1-inch piece ginger.

Wash the mutton in vinegar. Prick with a fork. Rub with salt and keep under a heavy weight for 24 hours. Grind all whole spices in vinegar. Slice ginger and garlic finely. Wash the mutton again in vinegar and rub the slices on both the sides with ground masala paste. Place the slices in layers in a jar. Sprinkle each layer with ginger, garlic and peppercorns. Pour sufficient vinegar to cover the whole. Shake the jar from time to time. Within a week it will be ready. To serve deep fry the slices till crisp.

Mango Pickle

12 medium mangoes.
1 tblsp. fenugreek seeds.
3 tblsps. mustard seeds.
25 flakes garlic.
2 tsps. turmeric powder.
1 cup each of salt and chilli powder.
1 kilo oil.

Cut the mangoes into slices. Mix with salt and set aside 1 day. Grind the whole spices and garlic coarsely. Heat half the oil and fry the spices till a nice aroma comes out of it. Remove the mangoes from it's brine and mix in the masala. Put in a jar and cover with remaining oil. Set in the sun for 15 days.

53

Whole Lime Pickle

1 kilo limes.
100 grams salt.
50 grams garam masala.
Juice of ¼ kilo limes.

Soak the limes for 24 hours in water. Drain and cut
each into four without breaking them at the bottom. Stuff
salt and garam masala into the limes, pour juice on top
and sun for 15 days.

54

Sweet and Sour Lime Pickle

3 dozens sour limes.
1 big bottle vinegar.
1 cup salt.
4 cups sugar.

Boil the limes in water till they turn slightly soft. Drain out the water. In a separate pan put 1 cup water with 1 cup salt. When crystals form, add half the vinegar and boil for 5 minutes. Heat half the cup sugar till it turns into a brown syrup. Add the remaining vinegar stirring all the time and sugar and boil till the syrup turns thick. Add vinegar salt mixture and limes. Boil for 5 minutes. Cool and bottle. Use after 5 days.

55

Lime Chutney

12 limes.
¾ cup salt.
1/3 cup each of chilli powder and sweet oil.

Cut limes into tiny pieces. Mix with salt and store in a jar for 3 days. Grind the limes to a paste using water from the limes. Heat oil and add the above ingredients. Keep on stirring till very thick. Cool and bottle.

Coconut Chutney

½ *doconut.*
2 tblsps. tamrind pulp.
A big pinch sugar.
4 red chillies.
1 tsp. cumin seeds.
2 flakes garlic.
1 onion.
Salt to taste.

Grind all the above ingredients to a paste with very little water.

Pork, Chicken, Beef & Mutton

blended with salt and water till dark. Serve in a tall glass layer . . . with a nice apple in it. . . . Garnish salad leaves around it with tiny . . . a little celery, onion tea and cucumber.

Roast Suckling Pig

1 whole suckling pig about 5 kilos in weight.

Filling......

1 big onion, minced, Liver and kidney of pig, sliced finely.
250 grams fresh bread crumbs.
4 flakes garlic.
1-inch piece ginger.
4 red chillies.
4 cloves.
1-inch piece cinnamon stick.
1 tsp. cumin seeds.
1 egg.
1 cup sliced corriander leaves.

Heat 5 tblsps. butter and fry onions till soft. Put in the liver and kidney and cook till dry. Grind garlic, ginger, chillies and spices to a paste. Beat egg nicely. Mix in the ground paste along with the rest of the filling ingredients. Have the pig prepared and ready for roasting from the piggery. Fill the pig with stuffing and then sew the opening. Place the pig in a roasting tray. Brush the outside nicely with ghee and bake in a preheated moderate oven basting it frequently with melted ghee blended with salt and water till done. Serve on a large silver tray with a nice apple in it's mouth. Arrange salad leaves around it with thinly sliced limes, onions, tomatotes and cucumber.

Pork Sorpotel

1 kilo pork.
250 grams liver of either pork and mutton.
6 red chillies.
1 tsp. each of cumin seeds and turmeric powder.
3 cloves.
6 pepercorns.
1-inch piece cinnamon stick.
2 medium onions, minced.
8 flakes garlic, minced.
1-inch piece ginger, minced.
2 green chillies, minced.
1 lime-sized ball of tamrind.
Salt and vinegar to suit the taste.

Grind all the spices to a paste in a little vinegar. Boil pork and liver in water till tender and dry. Fry in 4 tblsps. oil till nice and golden. Soak tamrind in 1 cup water for 5 minutes and then squeeze out the juice. Heat 4 tblsps. oil and fry ginger, garlic and onions till the mixture starts changing colour. Add ground mixture and fry till the oil comes to the top. Add liver and pork. Mix well add vinegar and tamrind and cook till the gravy turns thick. This dish tastes better if it is eaten the next day.

59

Spicy Pork

1 kilo pork.
5 large onions, sliced.
½ tsp. turmeric powder.
8 red chillies.
½ tsp. cumin seeds.
1 tblsp. coriander seeds.
1-inch piece cinnamon stick.
4 cloves.
4 cardamoms.
10 peppercorns.
½ tsp. mustard seeds.
10 flakes garlic.
2-inch piece ginger.
4 green chillies, slitted.
250 grams baby potatoes, boiled and peeled.
¼ cup vinegar.
Salt to taste.

Deep fry the potatoes to a golden colour. Roast **and**
grind together all the spices, chillies, ginger **and** garlic
in vinegar. Heat 4 tblsps. ghee and fry the onions to **a**

74

golden colour.　Add pork and spices.　Cook till the
pork is golden in colour.　Cover with hot water.　When
the pork is tender and the gravy thick, mix in the potatoes.　Serve hot.

golden colour. Add pork and spices. Cook till the pork is golden in colour. Cover with hot water. When the pork is tender add the gravy thick turn in the pork once more first

60

Pork Vindaloo

1 kilo pork.
¼ cup vinegar.
2 tblsps. tamrind juice.
1 tblsp. sugar.
12 red chillies.
12 flakes garlic.
1 tsp. cumin seeds.
½ tsp. turmeric powder.
5 big onions.
2-inch piece ginger.
½ tsp. peppercorns.
6 green chillies, slitted.
Salt to taste.

Grind 6 flakes garlic, half the ginger, red chillies and whole spices to a paste. Heat 4 tblsps. ghee and fry the onions, remaining ginger and garlic to a light golden colour. Add pork, ground spices and salt and fry nicely. Cover with hot water and cook till the pork is almost done. Mix in the remaining spices. When the pork is tender and gravy thick remove from fire.

61

Chicken Fried

1 chicken, disjointed.
1 tsp. cumin seeds.
4 cloves.
1 tsp. cinnamon stick.
10 peppercorns.
6 red chillies.
2-inch piece ginger.
10 flakes garlic.
1 tsp. turmeric powder.
1 tblsp. vinegar.
3 large tomatoes, peeled and sliced.
2 big potatoes.
Handful coriander leaves.
Salt to taste.

Peel the potatoes and cut into long thick fingers. Fry till they start changing colour. Cool. Mix in salt and fry them once again till crisp and golden. Grind all the spices with ginger and garlic to a paste. Mix the paste with salt and vinegar and apply on the chicken. Set aside for 1 hour, then put the chicken and 1 cup water in a pan and cook over a slow fire till tender and dry. Pour in 3 tblsps. oil and fry till red. Add tomatoes and cook till the tomatoes turn tender and gravy thick. Serve the chicken surrounded by potatotes and decorated with coriander leaves.

62

Chicken Chacooty

1 big chicken, jointed.
2 coconuts.
12 red chillies.
2 tsps. each of anise and coriander seeds.
1 tblsp. cumin seeds.
6 flakes garlic.
8 peppercorns.
1 tsp. fenugreek seeds.
½ tsp. grated nutmeg.
2 tblsps. poppy seeds.
6 big onions.
1 lime-sized ball of tamrind.
2 tblsps. vinegar.
Salt to suit the taste.

Fry all the spices and chillies in little oil till red. Then grind to a paste. Grate 1 coconut then fry with poppy seeds and 3 onions in oil to a golden colour and grind to a smooth paste. Extract 3 cups thin and 1 cup thick milk from the remaining coconut. Cover tamrind with hot water for 5 minutes then extract the juice. Heat 4 tblsps. each of ghee and sweet oil and fry the remaining onions to a golden colour. Add chicken, salt, spices and ground coconut. Mix nicely and then pour in the thin coconut milk and cook till the chicken is almost done. Put in the tamrind and continue cooking till the chicken is tender and gravy thick. Mix in the vinegar and thick coconut milk and heat nicely. Remove from fire and serve decorated with coriander leaves.

63

Beef Curry

1 kilo beef.
1 tsp. pepper.
1 tsp. garam masala.
1 tsp. ground cumin seeds.
1 tblsp. coriander powder.
7 red chillies.
6 flakes garlic.
¼ cup vinegar.
1-inch piece ginger.
½ tsp. turmeric powder.
250 grams baby potatoes, boiled and fried.
1 large onion, minced.
½ cup coriander leaves.
Few mint leaves.
4 green chillies, slitted.
150 grams tomatoes.
Salt to taste.

Grind the chillies, garlic and ginger in vinegar. Mix
together the ground paste, all the spices and beef. Cover
with hot water and cook till the beef is soft. Remove
from the gravy and fry in little oil to a golden colour.
Cut into pieces. Heat 4 tblsps. oil and add onion and

81

fry till soft. Add the tomatoes and cook till soft and dry. Put in the green leaves and chillies. Mix well and add the gravy. Cook for 5 minutes. Put beef and potatoes in a serving plate and pour the gravy on top.

64

Beef Roast

1 kilo beef.
½ cup vinegar.
3 whole potatoes, peeled.
3 whole carrots, peeled.
2 whole medium onions, peeled.
Handful of mint and coriander leaves.
8 red chillies.
1 tblsp. cumin seeds.
1 tsp. each of peppercorns, turmeric powder, garam
*   masala and coriander seeds.*
6 flakes garlic.
2-inch piece ginger.
Sugar and salt to taste.

Grind ginger, garlic and whole spices to a paste. Heat 4
tblsps. oil and fry the ground paste nicely. Add the beef
and fry to a red colour. Cover with hot water and cook
till the beef is almost done. Put in the vegetables, vinegar and sugar. Cook till the beef is tender. Decorate
with coriander and mint leaves.

65

Gravy Steaks

½ *kilo beef.*
¼ *cup vinegar.*
5 red chillies.
6 flakes garlic.
1 tsp. cumin seeds.
½ *tsp. turmeric powder.*
1 large onion.
1-inch piece ginger.
4 green chillies.
1 big tomato.
Salt and sugar to taste.

Grind onion, ginger, garlic, red chillies and cumin seeds
to a paste. Heat 4 tblsps. oil and fry the ground paste
nicely. Add beef and fry till the moisture is absorbed.
Add the spices, sugar, salt and tomatoes. Cover with
hot water. Put in vinegar and cook till the beef is tender
and very little gravy is left. Serve over boiled whole
baby potatoes which should be fried golden.

66

Trotters

1 dozen trotters, cleaned.
10 red chillies.
1-inch piece ginger.
8 flakes of garlic.
½ coconut.
1 tsp. turmeric powder.
2-inch piece cinnamon stick.
8 cloves.
A few sprigs coriander leaves.
4 onions.
1 tsp. each of cumin seeds and coriander leaves.
2 tblsps. vinegar.
Salt to taste.

Wash the trotters well. Boil in pressure cooker with 5 cups water for half an hour. Grind chillies, coconut, ginger, garlic and all the whole spices to a paste with vinegar. Heat 4 tblsps. oil and fry the onions to a light golden colour. Add the spices and fry till a nice aroma comes out of it. Add the trotters and the water in which they were boiled and 4 slit green chillies. Cook till the gravy is thick and the meat in dropping off the bones.

Head Curry

1 head of goat exclusive of brain.
1 onion.
1-inch piece ginger.
8 flakes garlic.
1 lime-sized ball of tamrind.
150 grams tomatoes.
½ tsp. turmeric powder.
6 red chillies.
1 tsp. garam masala.
A few curry leaves.
1 tsp. each of coriander powder and ground cumin seeds.
Salt to taste.

Clean the head inclusive of tongue, eyes, jaws and cheeks. Cut into big pieces and cook adding salt. After the meat is cooked, remove all the skull bones. Remove skin on tongue, palate and ear lobes. Cover the tamrind with water and set aside 15 minutes. Pass through a sieve. Heat 4 tblsps. oil and add the coarsely ground onion, ginger, garlic and curry leaves. Cook till the raw smell disappears. Add the tomatoes and all the spices. When soft add the meat. Cook for 5 minutes. Put in the tamrind and cook till the curry is thick. Serve decorated with coriander leaves.

68

Mutton Shakuti

500 grams mutton, cut into serving portions.
1 coconut.
1 tsp. cumin seeds.
1 tblsp. coriander seeds.
10 peppercorns.
8 red chillies.
1 tsp. garam masala.
½ tsp. turmeric powder.
1 tblsp. poppy seeds.
3 flakes garlic.
1-inch piece ginger.
2 big onions.
Lime-sized ball of tamrind.
Salt to taste.

Grind ¾ths of the coconut to a paste and extract thin
and thick milk. Fry the remaining coconut and all the
whole spices and grind to a paste with ginger and garlic.
Cover tamrind with hot water. After 15 minutes squeeze
out the juice. Heat 4 tblsps. oil and fry the onions to
a light golden colour. Add the mutton and fry to a red

colour. Put in the ground spices and thin milk. Cook till the mutton is almost done. Put in the tamrind. When the mutton is almost done put in the thick milk. Decorate with chopped corriander leaves and serve hot.

69

Fried Mutton

1 kilo mutton.
3 cups thick coconut milk.
10 peppercorns.
10 red chillies.
2 big tomatoes.
2 medium onions.
6 flakes garlic.
1-inch piece ginger.
1½ cups vinegar.
Salt to taste.

Cut the mutton into big pieces. Prick all over with a
fork and cover with vinegar. Set aside for 8 hours.
Grind together onions, ginger, garlic and whole spices to
a paste. Heat 4 tblsps. oil and fry the ground paste till
a nice aroma comes out of it. Add the mutton and
cook till brown. Put in the tomatoes and salt. When
the tomatoes are soft. Add coconut milk. Cook till the
mutton is soft and completely dry. Serve hot.

Mince

500 grams minced mutton.
500 grams onions, minced.
2-inch piece ginger, minced.
6 flakes garlic, minced.
5 green chillies, minced.
Handful of sliced corriander leaves.
1 tsp. garam masala.
1 tblsp. ground corriander seeds.
1 tsp. ground cumin seeds.
½ tsp. turmeric powder.
1 big tomatoe, sliced.
A few mint leaves
Salt and chilli powder to taste.

Heat 4 tblsps. oil and fry onion, ginger, garlic and chillies till soft. Add the mince and all the spices and cook till dry and crumbly. Add the tomatoes and mint and corriander leaves. When the mixture turns dry, add the hot water to cover the mince. Cook till completely dry. You can add peas to it when cooking and you can decorate it with boiled sliced eggs and fingerchips. This can also be used as a filling.

Mutton Royale

500 grams mutton.
Juice of 2 big limes.
6 red chillies.
10 pepper corns.
½ tsp. grated nutmeg.
4 cardamoms.
1 tblsp. poppy seeds.
1-inch piece cinnamon stick.
½ coconut.
2 medium onions, minced.
1 small onion.
1-inch piece ginger, minced.
6 flakes garlic.
1 tsp. cumin seeds.
1 tblsp. corriander seeds.
Handful of corriander leaves.
Salt to taste.

Grind chillies, ginger, garlic and all the spices to a paste.
Mix with lime juice. Apply on mutton and set aside for
half an hour. Dry roast the small onion and coconut

and grind to a paste. Heat 4 tblsps. oil and fry the onions till soft. Add the mutton and fry to a red colour. Put in the ground coconut paste and cover with hot water. Cook till the mutton is tender and dry. Serve hot.

Mutton Royale

500 grams mutton.
4 lime or 2 big limes.
2 red chillies.
10 pepper corns.
1/4 tsp. ground nutmeg.
6 cardamoms.
2 tblsp. poppy seeds.
1 inch piece cinnamon stick.
1/2 coconut.

72

Meat Rolls

500 grams leg mutton, cut into thin strips about 2-inches
*   broad.*
1 medium onion.
4 green chillies.
1-inch piece ginger.
6 flakes garlic.
Handful of corriander leaves.
A few mint leaves.
1 tsp. garam masala.
1 tblsp. ground corriander seeds.
1 tsp. ground cumin seeds.
½ tsp. turmeric powder.
1 bay leaf.
1-inch piece cinnamon stick.
4 cloves.
4 cardamoms.
1 cup curds.
150 grams tomatoes, sliced.
1 cup coconut milk.
2 medium onions, sliced.
Salt to taste.

Grind together onions, chillies, 6 red chillies, ginger and
garlic. Mix with ground spices and salt. Pound strips

of meat flat and spread some ground paste on each strip.
Roll into a tight roll and wind thread three or four times
around each roll. Mix together curds and coconut milk.
Fry the mutton rolls to a golden colour. Heat 4 tblsps.
oil and add the whole spices and onions. Fry to a
golden colour. Add turmeric and salt. Add the tomatoes and cook till soft. Put in the rolls and cover with
water. When the rolls are almost done. Put in the
coconut-curd mixture. Cook till the mutton is done and
gravy very thick. Serve hot.

73

Masala Livers

250 grams liver.
½ coconut.
1 large tomatoe.
1 medium onion, finely sliced.
1 cup shelled green peas.
1 tsp. garam masala.
1 tsp. ground cumin seeds.
1 tblsp. corriander powder.
½ tsp. turmeric powder.
1 big onion.
4 flakes garlic.
1-inch piece ginger.
Salt to taste.

Extract milk from coconut. Grind onion, ginger and garlic coarsely. Heat 4 tblsps. oil and fry the ground paste till the raw smell disappears. Add tomatoes, salt, spices and cook till dry. Put in the liver. When it turns dry. Add water and cook till the liver is almost done, put in the peas. When the liver is tender and dry pour in the coconut milk. Cook till thick. Serve hot.

Mutton Chacouti

500 grams mutton.
1 coconut.
3 onions.
4 red chillies.
1 tsp. each of cumin and poppy seeds and peppercorns.
½ tsp. mustard seeds.
1 tsp. garam masala.
4 green chillies, slitted.
6 flakes garlic.
1-inch piece ginger.
½ tsp. turmeric powder.
Handful of corriander leaves.
Salt to taste.

Grate and grind ¼ coconut and extract juice. Roast half the coconut with 1 onion and whole spices on a dry girdle to a red colour, grind to a paste. Cut the remainder coconut into pieces and fry to a red colour. Boil the mutton with 1 chopped onion, ginger, corriander leaves and salt till tender. Heat 3 tblsps. oil and fry remaining garlic, ginger and onion till light golden in colour. Add masala paste, mutton all the spices and milk of coconut. Mix well then put in 4 tblsps. tamrind juice. Cook till the gravy is thick. Decorate with corriander leaves.

Tea-time Savouries

75

Prawn Cutlets

500 grams prawns, cleaned.
2 small onions.
2 egg, beaten.
1 tsp. powdered cumin seeds.
2 flakes garlic.
½-inch piece ginger.
2 green chillies.
Handful of corriander leaves.
Bread crumbs. .
Salt and chilli powder to taste.

Fry onion, ginger and garlic in little oil till soft. Boil prawns in little water till tender and dry. Grind to a paste with the rest of the above ingredients with the exception of bread crumbs and eggs. Form into heart-shaped cutlets, roll in crumbs, dip in egg, roll in crumbs once again and deep fry to a golden colour.

76

Mutton Cutlets

500 grams minced mutton.
2 small onions.
2 green chillies.
½-inch piece ginger.
3 flakes garlic.
½ tsp. powdered cumin seeds.
1 tsp. garam masala.
2 eggs, slightly beaten.
A few corriander and mint leaves.
Salt and chilli powder to taste.
Bread crumbs.

Fry onions, ginger and garlic till soft in little oil. Boil
the mutton till tender and dry. Mix all the above ingredients together with the exception of crumbs and eggs
and grind to a paste. Form into round cutlets, dip in
egg, roll in crumbs and shallow fry to a golden colour.

77

Potato Rissoles

250 grams potatoes, boiled, peeled and mashed.
1½ tblsps. cornflour.
Salt to taste.
2 eggs, beaten.
Bread crumbs.

Mince filling . . . . half the quantity of mince as shown in the section on meat and use as filling.

Mix together potatoes, cornflour and salt and knead to a smooth mixture. Spread a portion of mashed potatoes evenly on your left palm. Place a tablespoon of mince in it. Shape into a cylinder. Dip in eggs, roll in crumbs and dip once again in crumbs. Deep fry to a golden colour. Serve hot.

78

Gram Special

Soak gram the previous day. Pressure cook till tender. Fry corriander leaves, green chillies, cumin seeds and chopped coconut in oil and add the boiled gram. Stir well and mix in the ground spices like garam masala, chilli powder and corriander powder.

Fish Cakes

500 grams fish, boiled and flaked.
1 egg.
1 tsp. ground cumin seeds.
½ tsp. pepper.
1 tsp. garam masala.
3 slices of bread, soaked in water and squeezed dry.
100 grams tomatoes.
2 medium onions, minced.
3 flakes garlic, minced.
½-inch piece ginger, minced.
Handful of corriander leaves.
4 green chillies, minced.
Salt to taste.

Heat 2 tblsps. oil and fry ginger, garlic, onions and chillies till soft. Add the peeled tomatoes and cook till soft and dry. Remove from fire and mix in the rest of the above ingredients. Knead till smooth. Form into oval cutlets. Roll in crumbs and deep fry to a golden colour.

80

Pan Rolls

2 cups refined flour.
2 eggs.
2¼ cups water.
Salt to taste.

For filling....prepare the mince as shown in the section on meat half the quantity.

Mix together flour, eggs, water and salt. Beat till smooth. Grease a frying pan lightly with oil. Pour a little batter into the pan swish it around and pour off excess, leaving a very thin layer of batter in the pan. Leave it on just long enough to set. When all the pancakes are made spread a portion of mince filling on a pancake, fold sides and roll into a tight roll. Moisten edges of rolls with 1 tblsp. cornflour mixed with ¼ cup water to seal. Deep fry to a golden brown colour.

81

Kangache Goss

Take half kilo of sweet potatoes. Boil till soft. Drain and grind to a paste with a little water to form a thick paste. Press through sev mould on a clean plastic sheet. Dry in the sun for 2 to 3 days. Store in airtight tin. When wanted for use deep fry to a golden colour. Drain roll in sugar and serve immediately.

82

Cones

250 grams refined flour or maida.
¼ cup milk.
3 tblsps. melted ghee.
Cone-shaped aluminium moulds.
Salt to taste.

Mix flour and salt together. Rub in ghee, add milk along with enough water to form a stiff dough. Cover and set aside for 15 minutes. Divide the dough into small balls. Roll out each ball into a thin sheet on a floured board. Cut each sheet into strips of about half inch in breadth. Wrap these strips around the mould. While wraping see that one edge of the strip is over the previous edge of the strip. Prepare a thin paste of 1 tsp. flour and 1½ tblsps. water and apply lightly to the edge of the strip on the top side (and not on the side touching the mould). That it may stick on the bottom edge of the previous strip. Take care that no water comes in contact with the cone. Heat enough oil for deep frying, then slip a few moulds into the hot fat. After a few minutes the cone will slip off the mould. If it does not slip off by itself, shake it out carefully being careful not to damage the cone. Remove the cones with the help of tongs and deep fry to a golden colour. Drain. Cool and fill with mince.... see section on meat. When cold you can use them with ice cream. They last a week in airtight tins.

Patties

250 grams refined flour or maida.
¼ tsp. baking soda.
2 tblsps. melted ghee.
Salt to taste.

Mix together all the above ingredients and add enough water to form a stiff dough. Divide the dough into balls and roll each ball out into a thin disc on a floured board. Cut into strips 4 inches in width. Place mince on one end of each strip and roll up into a flat roll. Stick down the loose ends with a thin paste made of 1 tsp. flour and 1½ tblsps. water. Deep fry to a golden colour. For mince.... see section on meat dishes.

84

Banana Balls

125 grams refined flour.
30 grams sugar.
Pinch of ground cardamoms and nutmeg.
1 tsp. melted butter.
Dash of salt.
4 ripe bananas.
Castor sugar.

Peel and cut the bananas into thick rounds. Blend together flour, salt, sugar and spices. Add enough water to form a batter. Mix in the butter and set aside for 15 minutes. Dip slices of bananas in the batter. Deep fry to a golden colour. Drain and serve hot sprinkled with castor sugar. Instead of banana you can use ripe mangoe or canned pineapple slices.

Pork Chops

½ *kilo pork chops.*
3 green chillies.
1-inch piece ginger.
4 flakes garlic.
Handful corriander leaves.
1 tsp. each of ground cumin seeds and garam masala.
1 egg, beaten.
Bread crumbs.
Handful of mint leaves.
Lime juice to taste.
½ *tsp. sugar.*

Grind ginger, garlic, green leaves, chillies and 1 small onion to a paste. Mix with all the spices and set the chutney aside. Steam-cook the chops. Apply chutney on the chops, roll in crumbs, dip in egg and roll once again in crumbs. Shallow fry to a golden colour.

Fried Brain

2 brains, boiled and cut into slices.
Chutney prepared as in the above recipe.
1 egg, beaten.
Bread crumbs.

Prepare the brain in the same manner as shown in the above recipe.

Rice Recipes

87

Mutton Pullao

2 cups Delhi rice.
500 grams mutton, cut into serving portions.
4 flakes garlic.
1-inch piece ginger.
3 red chillies.
1 cup curds.
2 big tomatoes, blanched and sliced.
50 grams cashewnuts.
1 big bunch sliced corriander leaves.
A big handful of mint leaves.
A few curry leaves.
5 cloves.
4 cardamoms.
½-inch piece cinnamon stick.
Juice of half a lime.
2 medium onions, finely sliced.
7 green chillies, slitted.
1 tsp. turmeric powder.
Salt to taste.

Grind red chillies, ginger, garlic and all but 10 cashewnuts to a paste. Fry the remaining cashewnuts to a golden colour. Pound together all the spices coarsely. Heat

6 tblsps. of ghee and fry the onions till soft. Add the spices, groundnut cashewnut paste, salt and mutton and fry to a golden colour. Put in tomatoes and curds. Cover tightly sprinkle water over the lid and cook over a slow fire till the mutton turns tender. Remove the vessel from fire and mix in the lime juice. Wash and soak the rice in 4 cups of water for 1 hour. Cook the rice in the water in which it was soaked after adding salt and turmeric powder till almost tender and dry. Mix in the mutton, green leaves and chillies. Cover the vessel with a thick cloth, then with a tight-fitting lid and place over a girdle. Cook for 10 minutes on a very slow fire. Serve hot garnished with fried cashewnuts.

Coconut Pullao

2 cups Delhi rice.
3 cups thin and 1 cup thick coconut milk.
½ tsp. turmeric powder.
2 cardamoms.
4 cloves.
½-inch piece cinnamon stick.
Salt to suit the taste.

Wash and soak the rice in water for 1 hour, then drain out all the water. Heat 2 tblsps. ghee and put in the whole spices and fry briefly. Put in the rice, salt and turmeric. Mix well, then pour in the thin coconut milk. Cook the rice till the liquid is almost absorbed, then pour in the thick coconut milk and continue cooking over a very slow fire till the rice is tender and dry. Serve hot.

Shellfish Pullao

2 cups Delhi rice.
1 large onion, minced.
3 large tomatoes, blanched and sliced.
2 hard-boiled eggs, shelled and cut into thin rings.
25 grams fried cashewnuts.
Handful of sliced corriander leaves.
1 tsp. each of sugar and turmeric powder.
500 grams shellfish.
¾-inch piece cinnamon stick.
4 cloves.
4 cardamoms.
3 red chillies, broken.
Salt to suit the taste.

Wash and soak rice in water for a few hours, then drain out the water. Wash and heat the shells without adding water, then take out the fish from the shells and set aside. Heat 4 tblsps. ghee and add the whole spices, fry briefly, then put in the onions and chillies and fry till the onions start changing colour. Put in the tomatoes, salt, sugar and turmeric powder and cook till the tomatoes turn soft. Add rice and fish and mix well. Pour in 4½ cups water, bring to a boil, reduce heat to simmering and cook till the rice turns almost tender and dry. Cover the vessel with a thick cloth, then with a tight-fitting lid and place it over a girdle. Cook over a slow fire till the rice becomes tender and dry. Serve hot garnished with cashewnuts, egg slices and corriander leaves.

1 bay leaf.
1 tsp. sugar.

boiled egg slices and coriander leaves.

90

Arrozo Fogade

2 cups Delhi rice.
4 cups mutton stock.
2 cloves.
1-inch piece cinnamon stick.
1 bay leaf.
1 tsp. sugar.
2 medium onions, minced.
2 medium tomatoes, blanched and sliced.
4 sausages.
2 hard-boiled eggs, shelled and quartered.
1-inch piece ginger, minced.
1 tblsp. corriander powder.
1 tsp. each of ground cumin seeds and garam masala.
Salt and chilli powder to taste.

Slice the sausages and fry them. Fry onions and ginger
to a golden brown colour in 2 tblsps. oil. Heat 1 tblsp.
ghee and put in the sugar. When it turns brown, put in
the stock. Mix in the whole spices, rice and onions.
Also add the ground spices. Cook the tomatoes till soft
in a tblsp. of oil and add to the rice. Bring it to a boil,
reduce heat and cook till the rice is tender and dry.
Decorate with sausages and eggs.

Tomato Pullao

2 cups rice.
4 cups coconut milk.
2 medium tomatoes peeled and diced.
4 cloves.
1 bay leaf.
1-inch piece cinnamon stick.
1 tsp. peppercorns.
1 medium onions, cut into thin rings.
Salt to taste.
½ tsp. turmeric powder.
12 fried cashewnuts.

Fry the onions till crisp. Finely slice 1 big onion and 1-inch piece ginger. Heat 4 tblsps. ghee and fry onion and ginger till soft. Add the whole spices. Mix well then add the tomatoes and cook till soft. Put in the salt and rice. Mix in 2 cups water with coconut milk and put inside. Put in the rest of the spices. Bring to a boil, reduce heat and cook till the rice is tender and dry. Decorate with onion rings and cashewnuts.

92

Kofta Pullao

2 cups Delhi rice.
1 cup shelled peas.
1 cup carrot sticks.
2 cups coconut milk.
2 large tomatoes, sliced.
4 cloves.
1-inch piece cinnamon stick.
2 bay leaves.
4 cardamoms.
2 rings canned pineapple, cubed.
12 fried cashewnuts.
For koftas......take half of the amount of mince as
prepared in the section on meats. Besides take 1 egg.
Bread crumbs.

Mix the egg into the mince and knead to a smooth mixture. Form into balls, roll in crumbs and deep fry to
a golden colour. Heat 4 tblsps. ghee and add the whole
spices and tomatoes. When the tomatoes are soft put
in the vegetables and rice. Pour in the coconut milk
along with enough water to stand 1-inch above the level
of the rice. Bring to a boil, reduce heat and cook till
the rice is tender and dry. Put the rice in a serving dish
and mix inside koftas, nuts and pineapples. Serve hot.

Vegetarian Recipes

93

Savoury Tindli

250 grams tindli.
1 medium onion, minced.
2 green chillies.
¼ coconut.
2 red chillies.
1 tsp. cumin seeds.
½ tsp. turmeric powder.
2 tblsps. finely grated coconut.
Handful of coriander leaves.

Wash and cut the vegetables into four pieces lengthwise.
Grind together chillies, coconut and cumin seeds to a
fine paste. Heat 1 tblsp. ghee and fry onion till soft.
Add vegetable and the ground paste, turmeric and salt.
Mix well, put in 1 cup water and cook till tender and
dry. Serve decorated with grated coconut and coriander
leaves.

94

Dal Masoor

2 cups masoor dal.
6 cocums.
3 red chillies.
1 tsp. cumin seeds.
1 tsp. coriander seeds.
½ tsp. turmeric powder.
4 flakes garlic, sliced.
¼ coconut.
1 onion, finely sliced.
Salt to taste.

Grind chillies, coconut, cumin and coriander seeds to a fine paste. Wash and soak dal in 6 cups of water for 2 hours. Heat 1 tblsp. oil and fry onion and garlic till soft, put in the ground paste and fry for 5 minutes. Add salt, turmeric powder and dal along with the water in which it was soaked. Bring to a boil, reduce heat to simmering, then put in cleaned and washed cocums. Cook till done. Serve hot with plain boiled rice.

Bittergourd Treat

500 grams prawns, cleaned.
500 grams bittergourds.
250 grams onions.
3 green chillies, minced.
1 tsp. turmeric powder.
1-inch piece ginger.
4 flakes garlic.
6 red chillies.
1 tsp. cumin seeds.
1 lime-sized ball of tamrind.
100 grams finely grated jaggery.
Salt to taste.

Soak tamrind in 1 cup water for 5 minutes and squeeze out the pulp. Remove bitterness from bittergourds after peeling and cutting them into thin rounds. For removing their bitterness sprinkle them with salt liberally and set aside whole night. Next morning, wash them in plenty of water. Slice onions finely. Grind to a paste chillies, ginger, garlic and cumin seeds. Heat 1 tblsp. ghee and 2 tblsps. coconut oil and fry the onions till almond coloured. Put in the ground paste, turmeric and salt and fry till a nice smell comes out of it. Add prawns and cook till dry. Then put in the bittergourds and enough water to cover the prawns and gourds and cook till almost done. Mix in jaggery and tamrind water and cook till done and the mixture turns quite thick. Serve hot garnished with coriander leaves.

96

Spinach Fried

2 bunches spinach, cleaned and sliced.
2 medium onions, sliced.
¼ finely grated coconut.
2 tblsps. masoor dal.
2 green chillies, minced.
1-inch piece ginger, minced.
Salt and chilli powder to taste.

Soak dal in water for a couple of hours, drain out the water and set aside. Heat 1 tblsp. oil and fry onion, ginger and chillies till soft. Put in the rest of the ingredients with the exception of coconut. Mix well add ½ tsp. turmeric powder. Cover tightly and cook over a slow fire adding little water till the spinach and dal is done. Mash coarsely, put in the coconut and remove from fire. Serve hot.

Brinjals in Coconut Milk

1 big brinjal.
1 medium onion, minced.
2 green chillies, minced.
1-inch piece ginger, minced.
1 cup coconut milk.
1 tblsp. ground coconut.
Salt and vinegar to suit the taste.

Roast brinjal over fire till the skin turns completely black. Toss in cold water. When cool, remove peel and mash to a pulp. Heat 1 tblsp. oil and fry ground coconut, onion, ginger and chillies till the mixture starts changing colour. Put in brinjal, coconut milk, salt, vinegar and chilli powder to taste. Cook till the mixture turns thick. Serve immediately.

98

Egg Vindaloo

8 hard boiled eggs, shelled.
4 flakes garlic.
½ inch piece ginger.
1 tsp. cumin seeds.
1 tsp. garam masala.
5 tblsps. vinegar.
1 tblsp. grated jaggery.
Salt to taste.
1 medium onion, sliced.
Handful of sliced coriander leaves.

Grind together chillies, garlic, ginger and cumin seeds. Crush jaggery and mix in vinegar. Fry eggs to a brown colour in oil. Heat 4 tblsps. oil and fry onions to light golden colour. Add ground paste and fry till the raw smell disappears. Add vinegar, ¾ cup hot water and the ground spices. Bring to a boil and put in the eggs. Cook till the gravy turns thick. Decorate with coriander leaves.

Masala Potatoes

6 *medium potatoes, peeled and cubed.*
1 *large onion.*
1 *large tomato.*
A *pinch of sugar.*
4 *red chillies.*
½ *tsp. ground cumin seeds.*
4 *flakes garlic.*
½-*inch piece ginger.*
Handful *of coriander leaves.*

Grind garlic, ginger, chillies, coriander leaves and onions to a paste. Heat 3 tblsps. oil and put in ½ tsp. cumin seeds. When it stops popping, add the tomatoes and fry till soft. Put in the potatoes. Mix well and cover with 1 cup water. Cook till tender and dry. Decorate with crisply fried onions, fried cashewnuts and raisins.

Egg Curry

6 *hard-boiled eggs.*
½ *coconut, grated.*
4 *red chillies.*
1 *medium onion, minced.*
4 *flakes garlic.*
¼-*inch piece ginger.*
1 *big tomato.*
1 *tsp. ground cumin seeds.*
1 *tblsp. coriander powder.*
½ *tsp. turmeric powder.*
Handful coriander leaves.
2 *tblsps. tamrind juice.*
Salt to taste.

Grind coconut, chillies, ginger, garlic and mix with ground spices and tamrind. Heat 3 tblsps. oil and fry the onions till soft. Add the ground paste and tomatoes and fry. Pour in 2 cups water, bring to a boil, reduce heat and put in the eggs. When the gravy turns thick remove from fire. Decorate with pineapple pieces, fried cashewnuts and coriander leaves.

101

Vegetable Curry

*500 grams mixed sliced vegetables like carrots, french
  beans, peas, cauliflower.*
½ coconut, grated.
1 cup each mint and coriunder leaves.
3 green chillies, chopped.
½-inch piece ginger.
2 flakes garlic.
1 tsp. ground cumin seeds.
1 tblsp. coriander powder.
½ tsp. turmeric powder.
Lime-size ball of tamrind.
1 large onion, minced.
100 grams tomatoes, sliced.
Salt and chilli powder to taste.

Grind coconut, ginger, garlic, chillies and green leaves
to a paste. Cover tamrind with hot water for 15 minutes
and then strain out the juice. Heat 4 tblsps. oil and
fry the onions till soft. Add the vegetables and fry
for 2 minutes. Put in tomatoes and coconut paste.
Cook till the tomatoes and vegetables are almost cooked. Add tamrind and ½ cup water. When the vegetables
are tender and gravy thick remove from fire and serve
with boiled rice.

102

Mango Curry

4 big green mangoes.
2 cloves.
2 cardamoms.
½-inch piece cinnamon stick.
1 tsp. cumin seeds.
4 red chillies.
125 grams jaggery.
Salt to taste.

Pound all the spices. Dissolve the jaggery in 2 cups water and strain. Peel and slice the mangoes. Do not discard the seed stones. Boil mangoes with 2 cups water when soft, add spices and jaggery. Cook till the curry turns quite thick. The seed stone is sucked after dipping it in gravy and it tastes delicious.